Monica —

you will
know how much
this means to me

John

Also by John Yamrus

78 RPM
Keep The Change
New And Used
Start To Finish
Someone Else's Dreams (novel)
Something
Poems
Those
Coming Home
American Night
15 Poems
Heartsongs
Lovely Youth (novel)
I Love

One Step at a Time

John Yamrus

PublishAmerica
Baltimore

ISBN: 1-4137-9857-8
PUBLISHED BY PUBLISHAMERICA, LLLP
www.publishamerica.com
Baltimore

Printed in the United States of America

for Kathy

Introduction

by Anita Wynn

I've never met John Yamrus in person. Wouldn't know the man from Father Adam if I passed him in the street. But, we've been corresponding for a while, now. He reads my poems. Sometimes, I get lucky, and I get to read his…

Being the age I am, I was able to grow into John's poetry. (Oh, yes, I've been a fan for years…) As I grew in understanding, he grew in ability, so we've kept pace for far longer than we've been corresponding.

You may ask yourself why I never refer to John's "work", but always John's "poems". It is for this reason:

John's poems are not work. I can tell you that John writes not because it's what he DOES, but because it's who he IS.

There are a lot of people these days who write poems. Poetry of all grades. Libidinous lovers who drip syrupy, sentimental quatrains. Angry young men, and women, who bludgeon us over the head with deliberate obscurity. These people use poetry as catharsis. They are not Poets.

> "…they're teachers
> or housewives
> or whatever
> and they write
> a little poetry
> because they all

fell for that line
about everyone
having a book in them.
They all try it
and they all end up
giving it up…" **

except him. He's still writing. STILL. WRITING.

John writes because he can't NOT write. It's his blood, his pneuma, his manna. If you told him, "John, no more writing," he would, being the nice guy he is, go quietly, but unmistakably, mad as a Hatter.

He Sees, you see. That's what a Poet does. Some of them rip the veil in two, and grab the back of our head, and force us to face their version of Reality. John lifts the curtain aside, and invites us to look. He takes an instant, shaves it clean of fuzzy perceptions, and hands it to us gently, saying, "See? Do you see?" No masks here. No fancy footwork. No fierce muscled obscurity. Just the same things you and I see every day, shorn of their disguises.

John writes because it's as much a calling as holy orders. He writes because he HAS to. Because he couldn't imagine his life without it. Some people write poems, and some people are POETS. John is one of the latter. The inheritor of a mantle left behind by a generation of poets we call The Beats. He said to me once "…Son of the Beats…" That's Truth, my friends. Son of Ginsberg, Kerouac, Ferlinghetti, and all those wonderful, strange men who shaped a generation, and as a result, all of the succeeding ones. A POET, by God.

**from: "i meet them everywhere," collected in the volume *Keep the Change*, 1992, by John Yamrus

(Anita Wynn, aka Autolykos, is a poet, author of *Speaking In Tongues)*

object lesson:

when looking in
the mirror,
it's often best
to overlook
the beginnings
of a sag
under the chin,
and the wrinkles
under the eyes.

it's often best
to ignore
the gray
around the temples…

and the
bloodshot eyes.

what
you've really
got to watch out for
is that look
of fear
and resignation…

even
terror.

it'll
kill you
every time.

i should be

cleaning the yard,
but i can't
bring myself to do it.

it's just
too nice out here…

all the neighbors
are cleaning their yards…

scrubbing,
digging, planting,
mowing…

i can
hear them at it.

and,
if i wanted,
i could
stand up
and watch.

but not now.

right now
it's just me
and the dogs
and a book.

and just maybe
we'll fall asleep
out here,
doing
absolutely nothing,
while the neighbors
continue their work,
getting ready
for the next
sunny day.

bullets

and
bombs,

knives
and poison…

guns, injection, the chair…

heart attack, cancer,
earthquake and
flame…

there's
plenty of ways
to go,

but the hardest and saddest of all

is
boredom.

after working in

the yard
this morning,
my hands smell like tomatoes...

they smell like grass...

they smell like dirt
and weeds...

they smell like
an old rubber garden hose...

they smell like mulch
and sweat
and gasoline...

they smell like
my father...

and his father...

and his.

walking hand in hand

thru New Hope,
we went into nearly every shop.

you bought a ring (the
guy who made it
said that elephants
were good luck)
and i bought a book of poetry,
a couple of cd's
and several bars
of handmade soap.

we watched the people
walking up and down the street.

we're no longer the
young ones.

the young ones
are Goths,
bikers,
kids with bright orange hair.

we held hands all day.

after all these years
we still hold hands…

more importantly,
more enduringly,
you and i
still
hold each other
by the heart.

a firmer grasp
there never was.

John Steinbeck

knew how to
write.

there was nothing
fancy
in the way
he laid down the words.

East of Eden,
Grapes of Wrath,
Cannery Row...

he didn't
show off
with the language,
he just came to work
and did the job.

i can go
on and on
about it...
the books,
the talent
and the true nobility
of just
doing the job.

it
must have been hard
being
John Steinbeck.

i called my mother today.

sometimes i call her
several times a day.

it doesn't matter,
because she forgets.

the only reason for me calling
is to make sure she's okay
and hasn't left anything
running
or burning.

it's only a matter of time
before we
have to make the hard choice
and move her into a
place
that'll be better for her,
but, will certainly be the death of her.

so, today,
when i called her,
i asked what she was doing
and she said
"waiting"…

i was afraid to ask
"for what?"

tonight

i'm watching the ballgame
(the Phillies are down
2-1 in the 7th)...

between innings i'm also
watching
The Sands Of Iwo Jima,
with John Wayne
and reading the poems of
Edna St. Vincent Millay.

one day,
between the poems
and the movies
and the ballgames,
death will surely
beat my door in...

before that time
i hope to
read
and write
and hope and love
and walk the streets at night.

one day, surely,
death will beat my door in…

and when it does…

when my back is to the wall
i will still
wave my arms
and try my luck
at shouting down the wind.

the television news

carries the same
stories…

a plane crash
out in the mid-west;

some guy who
got pinned under a
tractor trailer
and lived;

a shooting
on the south side;

drug busts
in center city.

bored with it all,
i turn it off
and walk down the hall,

stumbling toward
eternity…

film at 11.

they don't like it

when i play Miles Davis
music.

they don't like it
when i play it
in the car,
in the house,
or in the yard…

they'd much prefer i play
oldies…
country,
R & B…

anything
but Miles Davis.

i suppose
it's always been that way…

people will always
try to tell you
what to do,
or how to
act.

i'm just glad
that Miles Davis
never

listened.

i spent the night

sitting in my chair
listening to this set of tapes
i bought earlier in the day…

old radio shows from the
1940s and '50s…

hardboiled detectives.

Philip Marlowe
Boston Blackie
Johnny Dollar…

tough guys who
knew their way around
a knife
and a gun
and a dame.

men who
talked fast
and walked slow.

men of wit
and courage
and charm.

for 3 hours
i listened…

and then,
tired,
i finally took
one last slug of beer
and walked out onto the back porch
to stretch my legs,
hoping that someone would be stupid
or foolish
or desperate enough
to try and sneak up
and slug me
from behind.

i'm a sucker for black and white movies

and salads made with oil and vinegar.
and crunchy garlic bread.

i'd rather sleep than work…
and read than eat.

i have a high tolerance for pain,
except for needles
and hangnails.

i love dogs,
hate cats
and slam the door on Jehova's Witnesses.

i like W.C. Fields, Groucho Marx,
fart jokes
and anything that has to do with World War II.

i've had 3 great loves in my life.
2 were dogs…
and the 3rd
is upstairs, laying on the couch, half asleep,
watching Dateline.

old records

with their skips
and scratches
and hisses
and pops

make me
feel good.

i don't know
what the reason is,
but whenever i hear
some group from
the '50s
singing about
true love
or unrequited love
or young love
or lost love

i feel good.

i feel calm
and complete.

i feel like it's
maybe 3 in the morning
and the stars are out
and the radio's on
and they're
just about
to play a song
by the one and only
Lee Andrews
and The Hearts.

driving toward Philadelphia...

i've got the windows up
and the radio
is on loud.

this morning
i don't need
the world creeping in on me.

i can hardly
bring myself
to look out the window.

and when i do, finally,
i see a curled up
brown and white carcass.

a dog.

his legs are
broken and his neck's
thrown back
in an impossible angle.

there's almost a sneer
on his poor
dead face.

i don't need this.

this morning
i need
Smokey Robinson
and The Miracles.

and the radio
won't go
any louder.

ultimately,
there is nothing sadder
or lonelier
than a dead dog
on the side of the road.

the phone rings

in the evening.
usually i'm
on the couch
half asleep and
it's somebody
trying to
sell me something…

"Mr. Yamrus?"

"Yes?"

"I'm calling for
Restwell
Memorial Gardens…"

or,
"Budget Window",
or
"Roof City"…

i used to
be polite,
but they just
wouldn't
go away.

so, now,
when they call
i act
crazy.

i do
everything i can
to get them to believe
i'm sitting there,
on a beat-up couch,
eating macaroni and
finger sandwiches.

"May I speak
to your wife?"

"No, she's
in the yard."

"May I
speak to her?"

"No, she's
IN THE YARD.
I buried her
there
last week!"

eventually,
they get the hint
and hang up.

probably to
either
quit their job
or
call the police...

then
(if i'm lucky)
they'll go home,
lock their doors
and curl up
on the couch
waiting
for the phone
to ring.

he died Friday night

without grace
or gallantry
or style.

he died
with a tube in his nose
and his arm
black and swollen.

one scrawny foot
stuck out
from under the covers.

it was raining outside
and his
nails
needed a trim.

just the facts, please

no purchase necessary
void where prohibited by law
just add water
plus shipping and handling
must be 21 or older
limited to two per customer
4 easy payments
and call within the next ten minutes...

inundated,
i walk downstairs,
open up the refrigerator,
grab a beer
and slowly drink it down.

even empty,
the can
is cool in my hand
and i sit down
in front of the tv
and fall asleep
dreaming
about
operating
heavy machinery.

after midnight

on any
given evening,
in no particular
order
poets,
madmen
and drunks
are all
looking
either
for mercy,
inspiration
or a
good movie
on tv.

for years now

my poems have been filled
with silence
and quiet times…
little stuff.

i find
i'd much rather write about
laying on the couch
with the tv off,
listening to my dog
work on a bone
while the clock ticks.

no great thoughts
or theories
or even
memorable lines.

just life.

paring things down.

stripping them to the bone.

minimalist stuff.

keeping that in mind,
i'm even thinking of
going downstairs
and getting rid of all my books
with the exception of
To Kill A Mockingbird,
a dictionary
and
The Grapes Of Wrath.

knowing
for damn sure certain
that in all things vital,

less
is more.

my uncle John

is dying tonight.
he's 85
and wasted
to nothing.

he's got
the shakes
and can't
keep anything
down.

his wife
didn't want him
to go into
the hospital,
figuring that
once he got in
he'd never
get home.

and she's
right.

now, they
all take turns
going to the hospital
and sitting
and watching
and waiting.

it's a
stupid
and useless
roulette…

the winner gets
nothing…

and the losers
get to go home.

an illumination of sorts...

life,
love,
death,
god...

all the big ones.

well,
today
i was in the car
when i think
i solved
one of the riddles.

i was stopped at a light
when i looked over
to my left
at a sign out front
of the D & J
Sandwich Shop.

and right there
for everyone to see
in big black letters
was:

"love is a gift from god
hot dog and hamburger $1.75".

a hurt that scars the landscape of the soul...

that line
flashed in my mind
a minute ago...

but i didn't know
what to do with it,
so, i let it go...

i got in the car
and drove
toward the market
thinking to myself
that some things
just are...

that's all.

like the memory
of three white roses
in a short blue vase
on a
winter afternoon.

in the post office today,

standing in front of me in line,
was this woman
who brought tears to my eyes…
she was buying a
short stack of money orders
made out to
the gas company
and the electric company
and the phone company.

she had on this sad blue sweater
that was all pills on the elbows
and neck
and wrists
and her blue knit pants
were stretched out
and saggy
and she was smiling this smile
that i've seen
(and given)
a million times before…
a smile that says
"i know you know
this is all my money in the world,
but i'm doing the best i can."

without even seeing it
i know what her house looks like,
and i know what her kitchen looks like.

i know her table and her kids.
i know her car and her yard.

i wanted to go up to her and hug her.
i wanted to say
you're doing just fine.
you'll be okay.

but, i didn't.
i just stood there
in my stupid suit and tie.

she paid the guy
in crumpled twenties and tens
and fives and ones
that she pulled out of her purse...

and when the guy said
"you're still short a dollar thirty five"
i wanted to hand it to him
and say shut up,
can't you see anything
with your heart
instead of your head?

but i didn't.
i just stood there
in my stupid suit and tie
as she paid
the dollar thirty five
and turned around
and smiled
and walked away.

today. Wednesday.
ah, me.

today

i wrote two new poems,
neither of which
were any good.

today
i also
found a pile of crap
in the yard,

and a
small red ball.

today
i went to work,
came home,
threw the ball
with my dogs,
had supper
and fell asleep
on the couch
for an hour and a half.

today
i filed my nails,
squeezed a pimple
and read a bit.

today i
polished my shoes,
got grease on my shirt
and finally decided
that i don't mind
wearing glasses.

today
i wrote
two new poems,
neither of which
were very good.

and this is
just another.

after work

i come home,
walk into the kitchen
and throw my wallet
on the counter.

then my pens,
my cards
and finally
my keys,
which
slide along the counter,
spin,
do a little dance
and finally
come to a stop.

some day

so will
i.

Bukowski's latest book,

published posthumously,
is not
up to
his usual standards.

in fact,
it's not
very good at all.

i knew it.

i just knew
that
sooner or later

he'd
eventually

lose

it.

message read

on a
license plate

this
afternoon:

I WUV JB

for all
the money in the world

i wouldn't want to be
JB.

poem to the legendary Johnny Ace

who accidentally killed himself
playing Russian Roulette
on Christmas Eve, 1954:

pretty dumb
if you
ask me.

i am not

a misanthrope.
but, i do not

enjoy crowds,
or small talk,

or making people
feel nice
or comfortable.

i do not enjoy
wasting my time
laughing with a fool
or horse's ass.

i would much rather
spend the afternoon
on a chair
in the yard,
reading Zola,

and listening
to the music of
my dog
snoring.

after a very good month

at the typewriter,
the poems
have finally
slowed down.

but,
that's okay.

stuff happens.

the glory
comes and goes.

nobody's
going to give
anything to you.

you've got to
go after it
yourself.

the trick of it is
to be there
waiting
at the typewriter
when it happens.

and if you
don't write it down
and show it to someone

then
shame on you.

on reading some of

my poetry,
this guy i knew
said "shit,
if that's
what you call
poetry...
i can do
THAT
anytime."

and he
pulled a pen
out of his pocket
and wrote:
"the birds
that fly over
my yard
in the summer
never bother
to land,
they only
shit in the pool."

then
he put the pen
back into his pocket,
smiled
and walked away.

they don't get it, do they?

not saying
more than
twenty words
to each other
the whole afternoon,
we planted and
hosed and
scrubbed
the entire yard,
getting the place
ready for summer.

when we were done,
your shoes
and jeans
were soaked...
my hands were sore
and my neck
was stiff.

we came in the house,
ate a salad
and fell asleep
in front of the tv.

this is the gift...

and i am
one of the few
lucky enough
to have solved
it's mystery.

when i walked into

the waiting room
at the dentist's

there was only
one seat open…

i took it,
grabbed a copy of *Newsweek*
and tried to hide my face.

but,
before i even
opened the magazine

this guy on my right
starts talking:

"…used to play guitar once.
years ago,
when i was a kid.
i was pretty good at it, too!"

knowing it was useless,
i put down the magazine
and turned toward him.

he was
an ordinary kind of guy.
maybe 50.

"it was a great way
to pick up women.

i met all sorts of women
when i was playing guitar.

that's how
i met my wife."

just then they called my name
and i stood up.

he reached for my magazine
and said:

"it's been years
since i played guitar.

now,
i play

second fiddle."

write the poem...

i read
somewhere
a long long
time ago,
that the secret
to writing
is getting down
and doing it,
night
after night.

that was
bukowski's greatness...
and kerouac's
and zola's.

anybody can
write a good
poem.

once.

anybody can.

the real
secret
is doing it
over and over again,
night after night.

write the bad poems.

write the poems
that start out
as good ideas,
but end up
vague and faltering.

write the poems
after a party,
howling at the moon.

write the poems
when the only thing
in your life
that's going right
is the fact that
the toilet
stopped leaking.

write the poems
out of despair,
humor,
longing,
regret.

write them
because your team
got their
overpaid
asses kicked that night.

write them
because they
didn't.

write them
because
it's the only thing
you were
born to
do
or want to
do
or absolutely
have to
do.

my dogs

bark at the neighbors,
bark at the UPS man,
bark at cars
and kids on bicycles.

they bark at the television,
the radio
and the stereo.

they bark at
the vacuum cleaner,
the dust mop
and the broom.

they bark at
anyone
who enters the house
uninvited.

and
when they're not barking,
they're sitting there
waiting
for something
to bark at.

good dogs.

Dignity

Johnny Cash
has it.

Rosa Parks
and Bob Gibson
have it.

Henry Fonda
and the legless guy
who sold pencils
on public square
in Wilkes-Barre
had it.

it's in Carson McCuller's eyes
and Steinbeck's prose.

it's in the mad footsteps of the damned
and the music you hear outside your window
at 4 in the morning.

it's in the way Johnny Unitas stood,
stoop-shouldered and calm,
like God folding napkins for the breakfast of
eternity.

my uncle Dutch had it...

it's not a condition of wealth,
nor
position in the world.

you
either have it,
or you don't.

and that pitiful,
dull, smug
outrage of a kid
in the hundred dollar shades
and the BMW
who cut me off on the highway today
never will.

i was sitting in the kitchen

reading Steinbeck
when
she called me
from the car.

traffic was a mess and
she was gonna be late.

i should have
opened my book
and started reading again,
but Steinbeck couldn't hold me.

i was waiting for the phone to ring.

there's tragedies in life.
wars. killings.
senseless stupidity.
poverty.
rape.
and a thousand million injustices.

but it doesn't matter.
not even Steinbeck matters…

at least
not right now.

misreading William Carlos Williams

the line
reads:

"the gods live
severally
among us."

but
i read it as:

"the gods live
severely
among us."

either way

the old man's
right.

time's chipped away at me...

numb hand,
bad back...

some mornings
i limp
and find it
difficult
getting into
and out of
the car.

but,
that's to be expected,
isn't it?

this slow
wearing down
of the machine.

and
here i am,
among the pawn shops
and shopping malls and
liquor stores
and supermarkets...

here
i am
growing older,
waiting
to take
my turn
at being
the crazy old guy
who shakes his fist
at passing cars

knowing that
there's not one thing
perfect
in the world

with the sole exception
of this
moment

and this

and
this

and
i've taken the time
to memorize it

and i'm taking it
with me
to my grave.

my friend and i

talk.

we talk
about baseball...

we talk about
the fights (most recently
we talk about
whether Joe Frasier
could take Sonny Liston.
he CAN'T. at least,
not in MY poem, he can't).

and always
there's talk
about the movies.

film noir,
science fiction,
horror...

we talk about
John Agar,
King Donovan,
Marshall Thompson
and Faith Domergue.

i say: "it's age"…
he says: "it's fate".

"no, that's Kismet"…

to which we both reply:
"RONALD COLEMAN, 1942!"

silly me

i'm
a pack rat.

i save
everything.

i must have
at least 250 pens
saved (just
in case...).

i've got
bits and pieces
of cable wire
and connectors.

curtain rods
from windows
in an old apartment.

dried flowers,
bricks,
bits of board.

i've even got
tacked up
on the wall
right in front of me now
a veterinary appointment card
from a dog
that died
two years ago.

god, i loved that dog.

it was summer,

over forty years ago.
there were 3 of us kids
playing
at a construction site
behind my uncle's house
when we found
a small bird,
trapped,
struggling,
doomed
in a pool of soft tar.

knowing we
couldn't save it,
we knew we had to
put it out of its misery.

Raymond
ran home
for his BB gun,
which he loaded
and aimed
very carefully
while we all
stood around,
watching.

fascinated.

waiting
for him
to pull the trigger.

when he did,
the pellet
imbedded itself
in the skull
of that poor,
twisting creature.

sure of ourselves,
and our mission,
we discussed
where to put the next shot,
which had
no effect either.

we poured
shot after shot
into the screeching animal.

it was then
that my father
came up behind us.

he looked
at each of us
with the closest thing to hate
that we had ever seen.

he ended it
with a rock
and walked away.

this memory
is old and dusty,

but that bird,

with its strawberry mouth
and flapping wings

never
goes away.

Bukowski's property

this poem
isn't mine these
thoughts aren't
mine these
sentences aren't
mine these
cadences
aren't
mine these
lines aren't
mine.

nothing
i do
or think
or write
is mine.
it's all filtered down
through you
Mr. Bukowski...
and i wish
you'd
come here
and
take it
back.

she works

on the production line
in a wheelchair factory,
dreaming of Proust
and Ginsberg
and what would happen
if Heathcliff
were to really
enter her life.

she keeps a web log
that's so wonderfully
crazy
and inflamed
that her co-workers
heads would explode
if they ever read it.

she's capable of
discussing
Ezra Pound and maple syrup,
door handles,
Jim Morrison,
Jim Beam
and Johnny Walker.

she's studied Michaelangelo,
read *La Belle Dame Sans Merci*
and can tell you the real reason
why Rimbaud
took that shot in the leg
from Verlaine.

she's razor sharp,
read *The Razor's Edge*
and knows that
me too,
is pretty much the same
as
why not?

she
dreamed of college once,
and more…

but life
got in the way.

and now
she works the line,
dancing
on broken candles.

happy
to be the one
who knows the sound
that one hand
clapping
makes.

i'm torn

between this poem
and the movie
on t.v.

it's about
a giant squid
attacking
this little fishing village…

in the movie
there's the
sturdy old
sea-dog
who knows what's what,
who
the monster is
and how to kill it…

but,
nobody listens to him.

certainly not
the land developer,
or any of his
greedy friends.

and then
there's the poem…

it's a poem about
decadence
and pimples
and sweat.

it's a poem about
rainwater
working its way
down the side of
a wall,
and
the reflection of a
streetlamp
in the
bathroom mirror
at 3 in the morning.

but, i'm weak…
too tired to fight with
the poem tonight.

besides,
there are

machine guns
in the walls,
the ceiling's loaded
with bombs
and the light
behind my head
is way too bright.

so, for tonight
at least,
i'll
kiss off
any chance
for immortality
and go back
to the t.v.
and
my squid,

understanding
that it's
getting to be
way too late
for either one
of us.

she loves daisies

i'm not very good
at remembering that.

on those
rare occasions
when i DO
bring flowers
it's usually
roses,
or
those 3 dollar bundles
from the market.

never daisies.

and never
at the right moment.

it's usually
for something i did,

forgot
to do,

or
could have done.

and
when it IS
daisies,...
when i'm
putting them
in a vase
and adding water,

i can't help
thinking
about

bees.

you

are
a bowl of popcorn,

a slim volume of poems

and laughter
during a moment of silence

you are
pink bubble gum,

a damn fool

and the only
person in the world
i care about.

you are
a clock with no hands,

a blue bedroom

and a
twenty dollar bill.

you
refuse to accept
the inevitable.

you own
way too many dresses
and you don't
shoot pool.

you are
as uncomplaining
as the sea.

ultimately,

no one
can put you
into words,

not

even

me.

"there's a poem in here somewhere..."

this friend wrote to me,
enclosing a copy of my letter,
suggesting i take a look at it
and turn it into a poem.

it was a letter about
a reading i gave
at the local women's club.

it was a great letter,
filled with
descriptions of
the antique overstuffed chairs,
coat racks,
ticking clocks
and the rays of sunlight
showing in thru
curtained windows
onto carpet
rubbed shiny
by who knows how many
now dead feet.

it talked about
the stage in back
and the hall
filled with vague memories
of 1930s dances,
with young girls
sitting with ankles crossed
in shy expectancy.

it talked about
everything.

all that,
and more.

but what the letter
left out
was the fact that
after the reading was over...

after i shook hands,
made small talk
and smiled...

i walked out,
down the steps
and onto the street...

just another Joe
headed home

after a good
day's work.

Printed in the United States
35170LVS00006B/139-192

9 781413 798579